Good Question!

Why Did *T.rex* Have Short Arms?
AND OTHER QUESTIONS ABOUT . . .
Dinosaurs

STERLING CHILDREN'S BOOKS
New York

STERLING CHILDREN'S BOOKS
New York

An Imprint of Sterling Publishing
387 Park Avenue South
New York, NY 10016

ISBN 978-1-4549-0678-0 [hardcover]
ISBN 978-1-4549-0679-7 [paperback]

Distributed in Canada by Sterling Publishing
c/o Canadian Manda Group, 165 Dufferin Street
Toronto, Ontario, Canada M6K 3H6
Distributed in the United Kingdom by GMC Distribution Services
Castle Place, 166 High Street, Lewes, East Sussex, England BN7 1XU
Distributed in Australia by Capricorn Link (Australia) Pty. Ltd.
P.O. Box 704, Windsor, NSW 2756, Australia

Art by Julius Csotonyi
Design by Ellen Duda

For information about custom editions, special sales, and premium and corporate purchases, please contact Sterling Special Sales at 800-805-5489 or specialsales@sterlingpublishing.com.

Manufactured in China
Lot #:
2 4 6 8 10 9 7 5 3
12/14

www.sterlingpublishing.com/kids

Contents

What is a dinosaur?

Lizards. Snakes. Crocodiles. Turtles. These are some of the reptiles alive today. Reptiles have scaly skin and use lungs to breathe. They have strong backbones to support their bodies and help them move. Most young reptiles hatch from tough, leathery eggs and look just like their parents, only smaller. The first reptiles lived on Earth about 315 million years ago. For millions of years they ruled the land, the sky, and the sea.

Airplane-size pterosaurs (**TER**-oh-SAWRS) soared through the air, diving down to snatch up fish and other prey. Three different groups of reptiles—ichthyosaurs (IK-thee-oh-SAWRS), plesiosaurs (PLEE-zee-oh-SAWRS), and mosasaurs (MOES-a-SAWRS)—ruled the world's early oceans. But the most famous group of ancient reptiles lived on land. We call them dinosaurs.

The word *dinosaur* means "terrible lizard," and some dinosaurs were huge, fierce, meat eaters, or carnivores. But many were gentle plant eaters, or herbivores. Dinosaurs that ate both meat and plants are called omnivores. Some dinosaurs, like *Tarbosaurus* (TAR-bow-**SAWR**-us), were as big as a school bus, but others, like *Hesperonychus* (hes-pare-**ON**-i-kus), were no bigger than a chicken. So far, scientists have discovered more than five hundred different groups of dinosaurs, and there are many more left to find.

A mother *Therizinosaurus* (THER-ih-**ZEEN**-oh-SAWR-us) defends her young against a hungry *Tarbosaurus*. These dinosaurs lived in Asia about 70 million years ago.

How do we know about dinosaurs?

Everything we know about dinosaurs comes from fossils. Scientists have found more than 3,000 dinosaur skeletons. These body fossils are the remains of creatures that were once alive. They show us what life was like millions of years ago.

Trace fossils tell us how ancient creatures lived. Eggs and nests are examples of trace fossils. So are footprints and tooth marks. Coprolites are trace fossils of dinosaur droppings, or poop. Trace fossils help us understand how ancient creatures moved, what they ate, and how they raised their young.

Scientists who search for and study fossils are called paleontologists. To find fossils, paleontologists go to deserts and other open areas of land. When they spot rocks that formed when dinosaurs were alive, they hunt for bits of bone and other traces of past life.

Once in a while, scientists find a giant skeleton. That's when things get really exciting! Workers use shovels, jackhammers, and even dynamite to break open the rock surrounding the fossil. Then they use smaller tools to carefully chip away rock close to the bones. Finally, they can lift the fossil out of the ground.

Workers wrap the bones in plaster to protect them as they travel back to the lab. Then the scientists study the fossil closely.

Fossils come in many different types, like this footprint set in stone, or this Afrovenator (AF-ro-vee-NAY-tor) skeleton.

For many years, paleontologists thought the first dinosaurs lived in South America about 230 million years ago. These small, quick creatures stood on two feet and spent their days hunting smaller prey.

Eoraptor (EE-oh-**RAP**-tor) was about 3 feet, or 1 meter (m), tall and weighed no more than 20 pounds, or 9 kilograms (kg). It had a long head with dozens of small, sharp teeth and a long tail. *Eoraptor* had no trouble catching lizards, but it was probably an omnivore, meaning it ate plants as well as animals.

Staurikosaurus (STOR-ik-uh-**SAWR**-us) looked a lot like *Eoraptor*, but it was twice as big and three times as heavy. The slim predator could nab medium-size animals and tear them to bits with teeth that chewed up and down and forward and backward at the same time. Wow!

Herrerasaurus (her-RARE-uh-**SAWR**-us) could grow up to 10 feet (3 m) long and weighed at least 400 pounds (181 kg). The sharp-eyed, fast-footed hunter had its pick of prey, including smaller dinosaurs.

Recently, scientists made a surprising discovery that changed their minds about where and when the first dinosaurs lived. After spotting some old bones collecting dust at a museum in England, researchers decided to take a closer look. It turns out the fossils belonged to an early dinosaur that had lived in Africa, not South America. *Nyasasaurus* (knee-AHS-a-**SAWR**-us) was about the same size as *Herrerasaurus*, but it lived 10 to 15 million years earlier. *Nyasasaurus* may have been one of Earth's first dinosaurs.

In this scene from about 220 million years ago, a hungry *Herrerasaurus* chases a *Pisanosaurus* (pye-**SAN**-uh-SAWR-us), a small herbivore, across a volcanic flood plain in South America.

Why are dinosaur names so hard to say?

When someone discovers a new creature, he or she wants to give it a name that scientists all over the world can understand. But some scientists speak English, while others speak different languages, like Spanish, Chinese, or Russian. In the 1600s, an English plant scientist named John Ray had an idea to solve this problem. At that time, everyone who went to school learned to read a language called Latin. Most students learned Greek, too. Ray knew that if people used Latin and Greek words to identify new creatures, scientists all over the world could understand the names.

The name *Tyrannosaurus* (tye-RAN-uh-**SAWR**-us) is made up of two Greek words. *Tyrannos* means "tyrant," and *saurus* means "lizard." The name makes sense because *Tyrannosaurus* was a terrifying dinosaur that could slay anything in its path.

Giganotosaurus (jih-gah-NOTE-oh-**SAWR**-us) has a three-part name that means "giant southern lizard." It was a giant dinosaur that lived in South America.

The longest dinosaur name of all is *Micropachycephalosaurus* (MY-kro-PACK-ee-SEF-uh-lo-**SAWR**-us), which means "tiny thick-headed lizard." The small herbivore, or plant eater, had a thick skull and lived in China about 70 million years ago.

Sometimes paleontologists have fun when they name dinosaurs. In 1999, Scott Sampson and David Krause discovered a ferocious carnivore, or meat eater, and called it *Masiakasaurus knopfleri* (mah-SHEE-a-kuh-**SAWR**-us NOP-fle-rie). *Masiakasaurus* means "vicious lizard." *Knopfleri* honors Mark Knopfler, the lead singer of the rock band Dire Straits. One of the band's songs was playing on the radio when the scientists found the bones.

Because *Micropachycephalosaurus* was about 20 inches, or 51 centimeters (cm), long and just 7 inches (18 cm) tall, the small dinosaur was always on the lookout for predators.

Were dinosaurs good parents?

Most modern lizards, turtles, and snakes lay their eggs in loose soil. Then they leave, never returning to take care of their youngsters. Scientists think many female dinosaurs did the same thing.

But some mother dinosaurs acted more like modern alligators. *Psittacosaurus* (SIT-uh-ko-**SAWR**-us) probably spent several days piling up plants to build a mound-shaped nest. She guarded the eggs until the little ones hatched. Then she cared for the youngsters until they could survive on their own.

Maiasaura (MY-yuh-**SAWR**-uh) means "good mother lizard." These dinosaurs lived in large groups called herds and nested together like penguins and gulls do today. The females laid thirty to forty softball-size eggs in nests that were made of packed dirt and plants. When the babies hatched, their moms brought them food and took care of them for up to two years.

Some small dinosaurs acted even more like the birds alive today. *Troodon* (**TROH**-uh-don) and *Oviraptor* (oh-vi-**RAP**-tor) sat on their eggs, keeping them warm until they hatched. Which parent was in charge of nest duty? Scientists think the devoted dads sat on the eggs while the moms hunted for food.

Maiasaura lived in western North America about 74 million years ago.

During the day, a mother *Tianyulong* hisses at the winged *Anchiornis* that is trying to eat her egg.

When did dinosaurs sleep?

Think about the animals around us. Chipmunks and squirrels dart around backyards all day long, but raccoons and skunks come out at night. We usually see deer and rabbits in the early morning and late afternoon. These herbivores spend the hottest part of the day resting in shady spots. It turns out ancient animals were no different.

By studying the size and shape of the eye sockets in dinosaur skulls, scientists have learned that dinosaurs such as *Tianyulong* (**TY**-an-yuh-long), *Anchiornis* (**AN**-key-or-nis), and *Eosinopteryx* (EE-o-sin-**OP**-ter-ix) spent their days searching for food and trying to stay safe. At night, these reptiles settled down and went to sleep.

At night, two Velociraptors chase a small mammal.

But *Velociraptor* (veh-**LOSS**-ih-**RAP**-tor) led a very different life. These fierce, sharp-clawed predators rested all day long. At night, they hunted in groups. Small, speedy, and smart, *Velociraptors* may have tracked down larger dinosaurs and attacked the giant beasts while they slept.

Large plant-eating dinosaurs like *Argentinosaurus* (AHR-gen-TEEN-uh-**SAWR**-us) and *Diplodocus* (dih-**PLOD**-uh-kus) were active most of the day and most of the night. They took a break during the hot afternoon. These giant reptiles had to spend most of their lives eating because they needed lots and lots of food to fuel their supersized bodies.

What is the most famous dinosaur of all time?

Tyrannosaurus rex, of course! When T. rex was discovered in 1902, it took the world by storm. No one had ever seen anything like it. The 600-pound (272-kg) skull was packed with dozens of jagged teeth the size of bananas.

When T. rex went on display in New York City, at the American Museum of Natural History in 1906, visitors couldn't believe their eyes. They were fascinated by the prehistoric beast—and they still are.

Paleontologists have now dug up more than thirty T. rex skeletons, and they're learning more about the ancient killing machines every day. T. rex was the size of a school bus. When it stood up straight, it was as tall as a four-story building. The fearsome hunter was fast and fierce with excellent eyesight and a good sense of smell. Nothing stood a chance against T. rex.

Why did T. rex have short arms?

Scientists aren't sure. T. rex stood on two legs, so it didn't use its arms to move from place to place. Each hand had two fingers with sharp claws, but T. rex grabbed prey with its teeth.

Some paleontologists think T. rex may have used its arms to carry food. Because its skull was so heavy, carrying food in its mouth could have caused the dinosaur to lose its balance and tip over. Carrying food closer to its body would have helped T. rex balance its weight.

T. rex takes on Triceratops (try-**SAIR**-uh-tops) in a fierce battle.

Was *T. rex* the biggest meat-eating dinosaur?

T*. rex* was probably the largest predator to ever live in North America, but paleontologists have found even bigger meat-eating dinosaurs in other parts of the world.

Giganotosaurus lived in South America about 95 million years ago. It was a little bit larger than *T. rex*, and it had the biggest head of any prehistoric predator. *Giganotosaurus's* huge mouth had fifty sharp, narrow teeth that could slice like razor-sharp knives.

Spinosaurus (SPY-nuh-**SAWR**-us) is the largest, fiercest carnivore ever discovered. It could grow nearly 60 feet (18 m) long and weigh as much as 20 tons (20,000 kg). The giant beast lived in North Africa about 110 million years ago. *Spinosaurus* had a long, narrow head and a tall spiny sail on its back. It probably ate fish and may have spent some of its time in water.

Were there small meat-eating dinosaurs?

You bet! You've already learned about *Eoraptor*, one of the earliest dinosaurs. At just 3 feet (1 m) long, it was always on the lookout for danger.

Microraptor (**MY**-kro-**RAP**-tor) lived millions of years after *Eoraptor* and was even smaller. Just 2 feet (0.6 m) long, the four-winged dinosaur looked a little bit like a turkey. It probably ate insects, worms, and other small critters.

Compsognathus (komp-sog-**NAY**-thus) was about the same size as *Microraptor*. The little hunter dashed along ancient beaches in search of lizards and small sea creatures.

This *Anabisetia* (Att-nuh-bee-**SET**-ee-a) doesn't stand a chance against a mighty *Giganotosaurus*.

What were the biggest dinosaurs?

The tallest, longest, heaviest dinosaurs belonged to a group of herbivores called sauropods (**SAWR**-uh-pods). They had small heads, long necks, bulky bodies, and long tails. The huge creatures walked on four legs as they moved through ancient forests in search of food.

What was the biggest dinosaur of all? That's a good question! Scientists usually guess a dinosaur's size based on just a few bones. Some scientists think *Argentinosaurus* may have been the longest and heaviest creature to ever live on land.

Using some ribs, a leg bone, and a few bones from the *Argentinosaurus's* back, researchers estimate it could have been 100 feet (30.5 m) long and weighed as much as 100 tons (100,000 kg). But some scientists think sauropods like *Supersaurus* (SOO-per-**SAWR**-us) may have been longer and *Puertasaurus* (PWER-tuh-**SAWR**-us) or *Futalognkosaurus* (FOO-tuh-LONK-uh-**SAWR**-us) may have been heavier.

Many sauropods lived in herds, so they could warn their family and friends of danger. Scientists think they could scare off predators by making loud cracking sounds with their whip-like tails. If these gentle giants stayed safe, they could live for more than 100 years.

Paleontologists have studied body fossils and trace fossils of sauropods to find out how they fed and what they ate. It turns out that *Diplodocus* often ate plants that grew close to the ground. *Camarasaurus* (KAM-a-ra-**SAWR**-us) probably pulled leafy branches off tall trees. By feeding at different heights, both dinosaurs could have enough food.

> *Argentinosaurus lived in South America about 70 million years ago.*

How smart were dinosaurs?

What are the world's smartest animals? Humans. Chimpanzees and dolphins are smart, too. All of these animals have large brains compared to the size of their bodies.

Brains are made of soft tissue, so they can't form fossils. But scientists can tell how big a dinosaur's brain was by studying its skull. It turns out that most dinosaurs weren't very smart, but some had more brain power than today's reptiles. Which was the brainiest dinosaur of all? *Troodon*. The small hunter lived in North America about 75 million years ago. *Troodon* used its intelligence to catch small mammals and steal other dinosaur's eggs.

Many sauropods had huge bodies and tiny heads, so it's probably no surprise that they were pretty dumb. *Brachiosaurus* (BRACK-ee-uh-**SAWR**-us) lived in North America about 150 million years ago. The giant herbivore could grow taller than a three-story building, but its brain was so small that you could hold it in one hand.

Stegosaurus (STEG-uh-**SAWR**-us) may have been one of the dumbest dinosaurs of all. The huge, heavy herbivore had bony spikes and plates growing out of its back and tail. Even though *Stegosaurus* had a long head, most of it was filled with bone. The dinosaur's brain was about the size of a walnut.

Stegosaurus lived in western North America about 150 million years ago.

How did dinosaurs protect themselves from enemies?

Dinosaurs stayed safe in all kinds of ways.

Quick, clever *Troodon* could outsmart its predators and then race out of sight.

Ornithomimosaurs (or-nith-uh-MY-muh-**SAWRS**) were fast, too. The ostrich-like dinosaurs first appeared about 145 million years ago and lived all over the world. They could speed across ancient grasslands at 30 miles, or 48 kilometers (km), per hour.

Microraptor's small size helped it stay safe. Because it needed less food than larger plant-eating dinosaurs, it could stop eating and hide whenever it sensed danger. Huge predators probably wouldn't have even noticed such small prey.

Ankylosaurs (ang-**KEY**-loh-sawrs) needed a steady supply of food, and they were much too big to hide. Luckily, they were built for battle. Ankylosaurs looked like tanks with four stubby legs. Their bodies were covered with thick, bony plates.

Sauropelta (SAWR-oh-**PEL**-ta) lived in North America about 110 million years ago. It belonged to a group of ankylosaurs that had bands of armor studded with spikes.

Euoplocephalus (YOU-op-luh-**SEF**-uh-lus) lived in western North America about 75 million years ago. It belonged to a group of ankylosaurs that had bony clubs on their tails. If a predator attacked, the prickly herbivore fought back. One well-aimed whack with its tail club could deliver a bone-crushing blow that sent its attacker flying through the air.

Every inch of *Euoplocephalus's* body was protected with bony plates. The dinosaur's super-strong tail could easily knock down a hungry *Daspletosaurus* (dass-PLEE-tuh-**SAWR**-us).

What happened to the dinosaurs 65 million years ago?

Imagine a place with inky black skies and freezing cold temperatures. When you try to breathe, you choke on the thick, black dust, and there is a terrible smell of dead plants and animals. That's what Earth was like 65 million years ago.

What happened? Scientists think an asteroid, a rock from outer space, hit our planet. Dust from the explosion filled the sky and hung in the air for years. The dust blocked out sunlight, making Earth a dark, cold place. Because plants couldn't grow, herbivores starved to death. Without them, carnivores died, too.

Seventy percent of all living things died, including the dinosaurs. But some animals did survive. With dinosaurs gone, they had more places to live and more food to eat. Over time, new kinds of reptiles, birds, and mammals developed.

Did people live at the same time as dinosaurs?

No way! The earliest humans walked the earth around 2.3 million years ago. By then, dinosaurs had been dead and gone for more than 60 million years.

Our ancient relatives shared the world with large herbivores such as woolly mammoths and giant ground sloths. They worried about being attacked by cave bears and saber-tooth cats. None of these larger mammals are alive today. They are extinct. Scientists are still trying to figure out why they disappeared.

At the moment of impact, the deadly asteroid sent a giant plume of dust, dirt, and steam high into Earth's atmosphere. The explosion created a 110-mile-wide (177 km) hole in the middle of the Gulf of Mexico.

Because *Archaeopteryx* had wings covered with feathers, it could chase after flying insects.

Are there any dinosaurs alive today?

Believe it or not, birds are the modern relatives of dinosaurs. In fact, *T. rex* is more closely related to a blue jay than to an alligator.

Most paleontologists think that birds are a group of dinosaurs that developed around 150 million years ago. *Archaeopteryx* (ar-kee-**OP**-ter-icks) may be the earliest true bird discovered so far. It lived in central Europe about 150 million years ago.

Archaeopteryx looked like a cross between a lizard and a bird. Like a lizard, it had sharp teeth and a long tail. Its body was covered with feathers, and it had wings. But each wing had three small fingers with claws on the ends.

Scientists think that feathers first developed to help dinosaurs stay warm. Over time, feathers became larger and dino-bird bodies became more equipped to fly. At some point, feathered dinosaurs got a split-second of extra "lift" when they pounced on prey. This gave them an advantage over other small dinosaurs and helped them survive. As their bodies continued to change, dino-birds learned to glide. Eventually, they took flight.

By the time an asteroid struck Earth 65 million years ago, many kinds of dino-birds lived all over the world. Some of them survived the disaster and developed into the birds we see today.

Compare the Dinosaurs

1 Maiasaura
2 Therizinosaurus
3 Triceratops
4 Troodon
5 Torosaurus
6 Giganotosaurus
7 Edmontosaurus
8 Euplocephalus
9 Tarbosaurus
10 Stegosaurus
11 Tianyulong
12 Herrerasaurus

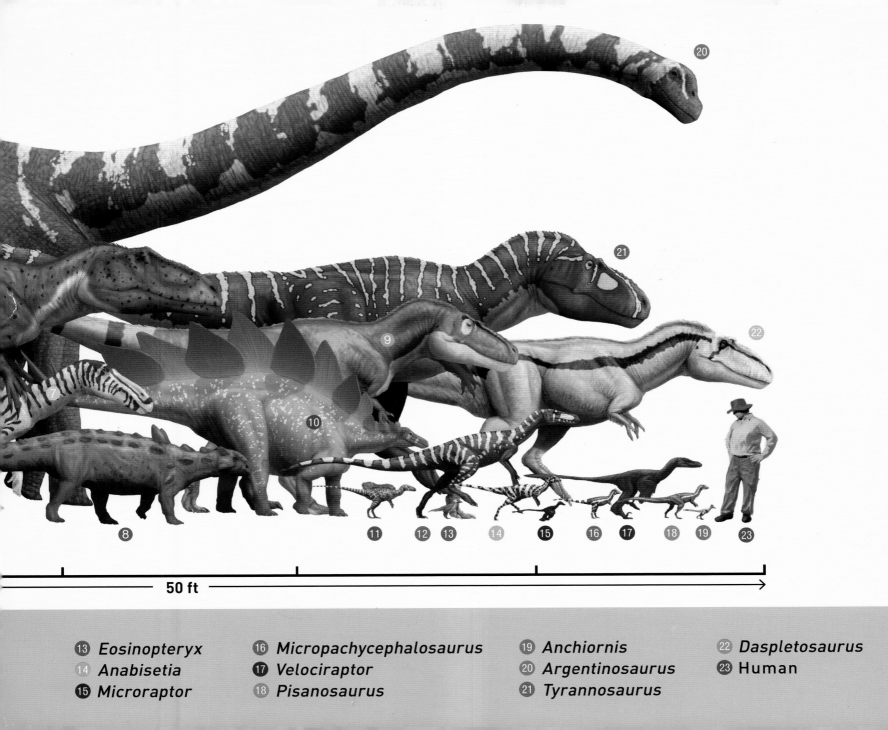

50 ft

Index

For bibliography, further reading, and free activities visit: www.sterlingpublishing.com/kids/good-question